IMAGES
of America

THE NAVY IN
NEWPORT

President Eisenhower at the Newport Naval Base, 1957. As official host at the Naval Base, Rear Admiral Henry Cromelin (left) escorts the president to a waiting helicopter which will take him to Quonset Point Naval Air Station. The president is accompanied by his naval aide, Captain E.D. Durand, USN. Afterwards, the president will board the *COLUMBINE* for the flight to Washington and conferences with government leaders. (Atlantic Fleet Camera Party photograph, courtesy Naval War College Archives and Dwight D. Eisenhower Library.)

IMAGES
of America

THE NAVY IN
NEWPORT

Lionel D. Wyld

ARCADIA

First published 1997
Copyright © Lionel D. Wyld, 1997

ISBN 0-7524-0471-7

Published by Arcadia Publishing,
an imprint of the Chalford Publishing Corporation,
One Washington Center, Dover, New Hampshire 03820.
Printed in Great Britain

Library of Congress Cataloging-in-Publication Data applied for

OTHER PUBLICATIONS BY LIONEL D. WYLD:

Boaters and Broomsticks
Low Bridge! Folklore and the Erie Canal
Walter D. Edmonds, Storyteller

Contents

Introduction   7

1. From Colonial Times to the Naval Torpedo Station   9

2. Torpedoes and Torpedo Boats   23

3. The Naval Training Station and Naval War College   43

4. The Navy in Newport: 1900–1940   53

5. The Navy in Newport in World War II   71

6. Postwar Consolidation and Change   93

7. Epilogue   123

Acknowledgments   128

Introduction

Known as "The City by the Sea," Newport, Rhode Island, has a long history of maritime activity. Early in the colonial period, Newport was recognized as both an important seaport for the mercantile trade and a harbor of inestimable value for naval vessels.

Today's Newport navy complex is situated on Aquidneck Island (the original "Rhode Island"), which comprises the city of Newport and the towns of Middletown and Portsmouth. While the U.S. Navy's original site in Newport was limited to Goat Island—where the pioneer Naval Torpedo Station was established in 1869—in the 1880s, the Naval War College (1884) and the Naval Training Station (1883) were founded on nearby Coasters Harbor Island. The navy's presence in Narragansett Bay expanded in the twentieth century through two world wars. In 1941, the U.S. Naval Operating Base, headquartered on Coasters Harbor Island, was established to coordinate the activity of all naval facilities in the area, including the Quonset Point Naval Air Station and the Naval Construction Battalion Center ("Seabees") at Davisville. The wartime operating base was disestablished in 1946 and replaced by a single military command for the area, designated the U.S. Naval Base at Newport. In addition to the Naval Torpedo Station on Goat Island, the Naval War College, and the Naval Training Station, the Naval Base at Newport included all component commands and area-coordinated commands on both sides of Narragansett Bay. From Newport, the East Passage included several small offshore islands and shore facilities that extended along the bay through Middletown to Portsmouth's Melville Point seven miles north. (This area is perhaps best known to history for its Motor Torpedo Boat Training Center in World War II and the motion picture *PT-109*, based upon the wartime naval service of John F. Kennedy as portrayed by actor Cliff Robertson.)

In the early 1950s, the Naval Torpedo Station was disestablished, and a new Newport Naval Station Command formed to provide logistic support to other naval activities in the region. Then, the Naval Training Station was decommissioned, and recruit training shifted to Bainbridge, Maryland. From 1967 to 1973, Newport was the headquarters of the navy's two-hundred-ship Cruiser-Destroyer Force, U.S. Atlantic Fleet, and over fifty ships were homeported at its Coddington Cove piers. In 1974, further peacetime conversion resulted in the consolidation of the Naval Base at Newport, the Newport Naval Station, and naval officer training. The Naval Education and Training Center was established, augmenting the missions of the Naval War College and other school commands in Newport. That same year, the Naval Academy Preparatory School in Maryland returned to Newport, where it had begun in 1915.

Just offshore from the city of Newport, the Naval War College and Naval Training Station continued to expand. The historic Naval Torpedo Station, officially closed in 1951, began navy research and development activities; the station's work continued through its successors, and in 1970, this division became known as the Naval Underwater Systems Center (NUSC). For over twenty years, it was a leading research, development, test, and evaluation facility for the navy; NUSC included major laboratories in Newport (also the location of its headquarters) and New London, Connecticut, along with a number of far-flung detachments at sites in upstate New York, Bermuda, Florida, and the Bahamas. On January 2, 1992, following recommendations of the government's Base Closure and Realignment Committee, it became the Naval Undersea Warfare Center Division Newport, continuing the work for which its predecessor organizations were so well known in the military and scientific communities.

The prestigious Naval War College, the Naval Education and Training Center, and the various navy command schools, with their large and diverse staffs of military and civilian personnel—comprised of some two thousand enlisted and officer students annually—also continued to keep the navy a leading employer in Rhode Island and southeastern New England.

The Navy in Newport takes a look at the navy's presence in the City by the Sea and provides a pictorial record of its colorful and enduring history.

Lionel D. Wyld

One

From Colonial Times to the Naval Torpedo Station

Newport in colonial times. This map of Newport in the Province of Rhode Island includes an early layout of the settlement, streets, and dock areas. Goat Island (in the center foreground) later takes on prominence as the site of military forts for the protection of the harbor and, still later, becomes the location of a post-Civil War naval station.

Newport harbor in the mid-nineteenth century. From early colonial times, Newport bustled with maritime activity, both commercial and military.

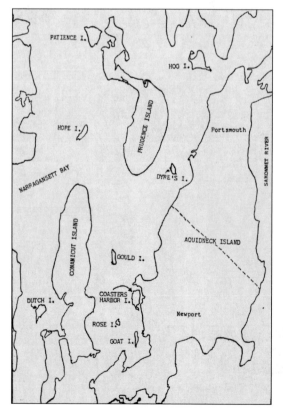

Islands near Newport. This map of Narragansett Bay near Aquidneck Island from *Newport Begins* by L.A. Robson (Newport Historical Society) details the East Passage and shows the relationship of Newport to Goat Island, site of the navy's first experimental torpedo station in 1869 and Coasters Harbor Island, where the Naval Training Station and Naval War College began in 1883–1884. Other nearby islands were used over the years by the navy, particularly during World War I and World War II.

Commander of the first navy. On December 22, 1775, Rhode Island's Esek Hopkins was commissioned the first "Commander in Chief of the Fleet of the United Colonies." Hopkins was thus commander of America's first navy. Esek's son, John Hopkins, was captain of the *Cabot* in the first Continental fleet; another Rhode Islander, Abraham Whipple, commanded the *Columbus* for the Colonies. (Brown University Archives.)

The *Katy*, 1775. A Rhode Island Navy sloop, the *Katy* became one of the five ships in America's first navy—the newly established Continental fleet. Renamed the USS *Providence* in the Revolutionary War, it was the first command of John Paul Jones. (*Newport Navalog.*)

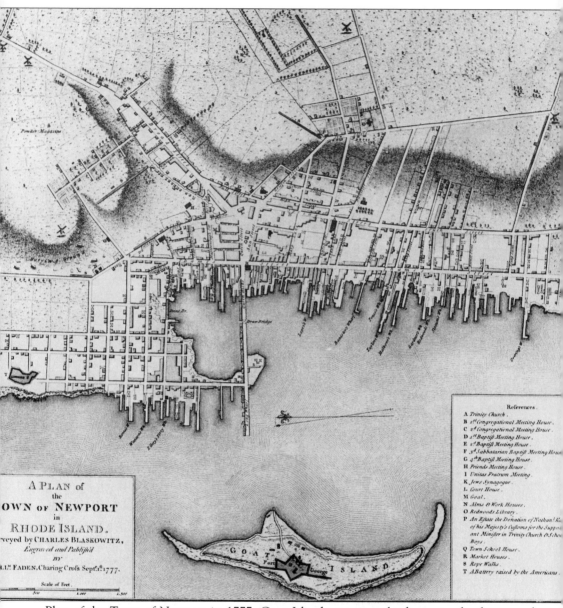

References.
A *Trinity Church .*
B *1st Congregational Meeting House .*
C *2d Congregational Meeting House .*
D *1st Baptist Meeting House .*
E *2d Baptist Meeting House .*
F *3d Sabbatarian Baptist Meeting Hous*
G *4th Baptist Meeting House .*
H *Friends Meeting House .*
I *Unitas Fratrum Meeting .*
K *Jews Synagogue .*
L *Court House .*
M *Goal .*
N *Alms & Work Houses .*
O *Redwoods Library .*
P *An Estate the Donation of Nathan l Ki*
   of his Majesty's Customs for the Suppo
   ant Minister in Trinity Church & Scho
   Boys .
Q *Town School House .*
R *Market Houses .*
S *Rope Walks .*
T *A Battery raised by the Americans .*

A PLAN of
the
OWN of NEWPORT
in
RHODE ISLAND.
veyed by CHARLES BLASKOWITZ,
Engraved and Publish'd
BY
J.Wm FADEN, Charing Cross Sept.r 1st 1777.

Scale of Feet.

Plan of the Town of Newport in 1777. Goat Island, prominently shown in the foreground, became the site of the first official U.S. Naval Research Station, established nearly a century later in 1869. Fort George (shown on the island) was set up in pre-Revolutionary times to protect the harbor entrance to Newport. It underwent several name changes reflecting the reigning British monarchs and political shifts in colonial times and the early republic.

12

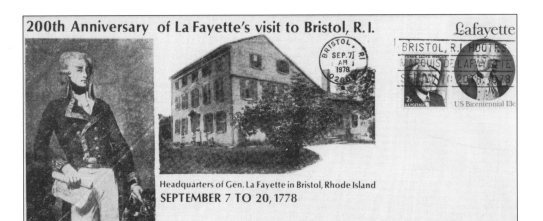

200th Anniversary of La Fayette's visit to Bristol, R. I.

Headquarters of Gen. La Fayette in Bristol, Rhode Island
SEPTEMBER 7 TO 20, 1778

LE MARQUIS DE La FAYETTE

General Lafayette in Rhode Island. In September 1778, the Marquis de Lafayette—whom the Continental Congress had made a major general at George Washington's request—took command of the ports within the Island of Rhode Island. Entrusted with the care of Warren, Bristol, and "the eastern shore" (Newport was in British hands), General Lafayette made his headquarters first in Bristol and then at "a safer place behind Warren." For the 200th anniversary (1978) of Lafayette's tour of duty in Rhode Island, Bristol artist R.V. Simpson created a commemorative cover. Franked with a Lafayette U.S. Bicentennial stamp, the philatelic item is shown here (in black and white) with a special Bristol cancellation. (Author's collection.)

Coasters Harbor Island, c. 1832. The offshore island where the founders of the City by the Sea landed in 1639 is two miles north of the center of Newport. In 1883, a Naval Training Station was established on the island, and the next year, in 1884, the Newport Alms House (shown above) became the first home of the Naval War College. The Alms House, an asylum for the poor, was built by Benjamin Chase of Newport, chiefly of fieldstone from the island, at a cost of $6,940. Work on the building began in 1817 and was completed in March 1820. (Naval War College Museum.)

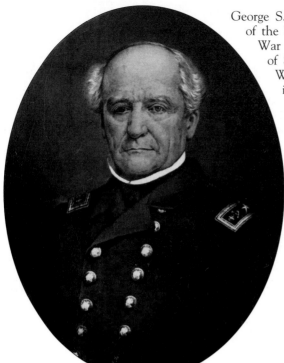

George S. Blake (1803–1871) as superintendent of the U.S. Naval Academy. When the Civil War threatened, Blake sought the help of Secretary of the Navy Gideon Welles. With secessionist sympathy fairly high in the border state of Maryland, Blake recommended prompt removal of the academy, staff, and students to a safer location. He also believed that the *Constitution*, assigned to Annapolis as a school ship, should be saved from possible Confederate capture and exploitation. On April 27, 1861, Secretary Welles approved the academy's removal from Newport, Rhode Island. (U.S. Naval Academy Archives.)

USS *Constitution*. This historic ship, known as "Old Ironsides" and assigned to the U.S. Naval Academy at Annapolis from 1860–1871, was used to transport midshipmen to Newport when the Civil War threatened. The navy also engaged the steamer *Baltic* to carry officers, civilian professors, and their families. The ships arrived in Newport on May 9, 1961, and received a 24-gun salute from Fort Adams. (U.S. Naval Academy Archives.)

The Civil War years in Annapolis. The U.S. Naval Academy served as a military hospital, and Union troops occupied the grounds after the staff and midshipmen were removed to Newport, Rhode Island, for safety during the war period. (U.S. Naval Academy Archives.)

C.R.P. Rodgers, a commandant of midshipmen at Newport. Upon arrival in Newport in 1861, Lieutenant (later Admiral) Rodger became academy superintendent in the absence of Captain George S. Blake, who had remained in Annapolis. (U.S. Naval Academy Archives.)

USS *Constitution* coming to Newport. In this view, "Old Ironsides," the ship that brought Annapolis to Newport in 1861, is moored at Goat Island in Newport Harbor during the Civil War. It returned to Annapolis in mid-1865.

Academy site in Newport. When the U.S. Naval Academy was moved from Annapolis to Newport, the navy selected Fort Adams—at the entrance to Newport Harbor—as the academy's site. Fort Adams had recently been vacated by the army, but barely half of the navy officers and faculty could be quartered within its old walls. The navy then leased a large, four-story hotel, the Atlantic House on Bellevue Avenue, for the duration of its stay in Newport. Officers quarters and mess were on the ground floor, classrooms on the second, and upperclass midshipmen billets on the top floors. Truro Park, then as now, provides a pleasant recreation area just across the street. This marker designates the site, now home to the Elks Club of Newport, occupied by the academy from 1861–1865. (Darcy Associates, Ltd.)

William Thomas Sampson (1840–1902) as a midshipman. A native of Palmyra, New York, and Honor Man of the U.S. Naval Academy Class of 1861, Sampson was an instructor during the academy's Civil War period in Newport. He later served as superintendent of the academy. (U.S. Naval Academy Archives.)

USS *Santee*. In 1862, the *Santee* arrived in Newport to support the *Constitution*, which was moored at Goat Island. It would serve as a U.S. Naval Academy school ship for the next fifty years. (U.S. Naval Academy Archives.)

Members of the U.S. Naval Academy Class of 1864 at Newport, Rhode Island. When the U.S. Naval Academy was removed from Annapolis, Maryland, to Newport during the Civil War, classes went on, and these midshipmen became the first class to graduate during the academy's stay in Newport. (U.S. Naval Academy Archives.)

Naval Torpedo Station, Newport, *c.* 1870. On July 29, 1869, the Secretary of War authorized the Navy Department to establish an experimental torpedo station on Goat Island, a 32-acre site in Newport Harbor. Commander E.O. Matthews was designated Commanding Officer and Inspector in Charge. This is the earliest known photograph of the Naval Torpedo Station at Newport. (Naval War College Museum.)

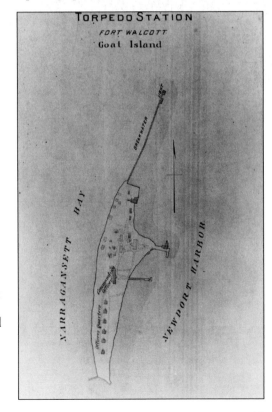

The Naval Torpedo Station, 1873. The first buildings on Goat Island were those formerly used by army personnel who staffed the old fortification. These structures were used by the U.S. Naval Academy that was relocated to Newport during the Civil War. The drawing appeared in *Harper's Weekly* in 1873.

Newport harbor in 1873. This sketch of the harbor, also from *Harper's Weekly*, shows the Naval Torpedo Station and Goat Island in front of the Newport shoreline.

INSPECTORS OF ORDNANCE
IN CHARGE
OF TORPEDO STATION.

COMDR....E.O.MATTHEWS,..........	JUNE 1869 TO JULY 1873.
CAPTAIN..EDWARD SIMPSON,.....JULY 1873 TO JUNE 1875.
CAPTAIN..K.R.BREESE,...........	JUNE 1875 TO SEPT. 16,1878.
CAPTAIN..F.M.RAMSAY,...........	SEPT. 16, 1878 TO JAN. 15,1881.
COMDR....T.O.SELFRIDGE,.....	JAN. 15,1881 TO NOV. 1, 1884.
COMDR....W.T. SAMPSON,........	NOV. 1, 1884 TO SEPT. 7, 1886.
COMDR....C.F. GOODRICH,........	SEPT. 7, 1886 TO NOV. 15,1889.
COMDR....T.F. JEWELL,.........	DEC. 6, 1889 TO JAN. 2, 1893.
COMDR....G.A CONVERSE,.......	JAN. 2, 1893 TO JUNE 15,1897.
LT.COMDR. T.G. McLEAN,..........	JUNE 15, 1897 TO OCT. 6, 1899.
LT.COMDR. N.E. MASON,...........	OCT. 6, 1899 TO JUNE 2, 1902.
LT.COMDR. F.F. FLETCHER,........	JUNE 2, 1902 TO NOV. 4, 1904.
LT.COMDR. ALBERT GLEAVES,.....	NOV. 16, 1904 TO APR. 10,1908.
LT.COMDR. MARK L. BRISTOL,......	JUNE 17, 1908 TO MAY 8,1911.
COMDR....C.W.WILLIAMS,.......	MAY 8,1911 TO MAR.26,1914.
COMDR....JOHN K.ROBISON,......	MAR.26,1914 TO MAR.26,1917.
CAPTAIN..EDWARD L.BEACH,......	MAR.26,1917 TO SEPT.12,1918.
CAPTAIN..MARTIN E.TRENCH,....	SEPT.12,1918 TO SEPT.24,1920.
CAPTAIN..THOMAS J.SENN........	OCT. 2, 1920 TO MAR. 15,1923.
CAPTAIN..RALPH EARLE,........	MAY 26, 1923 TO MAY 25,1925.
CAPTAIN..EDGAR B.LARIMER....	MAY 25, 1925 TO OCT. 4,1927.
CAPTAIN..THOS. C.HART,...........	OCT. 4, 1927 TO JUNE 17,1929.
CAPTAIN..JOSEPH R.DEFREES....	JULY 17,1929 TO JUNE 15,1931.
CAPTAIN..FRANK L.PINNEY.......	JUNE 15,1931 TO JUNE29,1933.
CAPTAIN..HARVEY DELANO,.......	JUNE29, 1933 TO JUNE25,1935.
CAPTAIN..ISAAC C JOHNSON......	JUNE25, 1935 TO APR. 29,1939.
CAPTAIN..THOMAS WITHERS......	MAY 10, 1939 TO JAN 2,1941
CAPTAIN..FRANK H.ROBERTS.....	FEB. 8, 1941 TO FEB. 6,1943.
CAPTAIN..FRANK G.FAHRION......	FEB. 6,1943 TO APR. 17,1943.

Naval Torpedo Station commanders. This plaque lists the names of the military commanders of the Naval Torpedo Station from its inception in 1869 to its disestablishment in 1951. For over seventy years, from 1869 to 1943, this commanding officer was designated "Inspector of Ordnance in Charge." The title was changed to "Commanding Officer" beginning in 1943. A second plaque (not shown) carries the names of the commanding officers of successor organizations, the Naval Underwater Ordnance Station (1951–1966) and Naval Underwater Weapons Research and Engineering Station (1966–1970).

Goat Island, c. 1876. The Navy Department's first experimental torpedo facility grew rapidly in the first decade after its establishment in Newport harbor in 1869. Later, the Naval Torpedo Station saw heightened activity through two world wars. In the early 1940s, particularly, both its technical research activity and production capacity were expanded to support the fleet. (Naval War College Museum.)

Two
Torpedoes and Torpedo Boats

East Dock, Goat Island, 1899. The tug *Leyden* ties up at the Naval Torpedo Station ferry landing, where three early torpedo boats are already docked.

Naval Torpedo Station at the turn of the century. This view of Goat Island shows torpedo boats USS *Cushing* and USS *Porter* at the piers (left) and torpedo boat USS *Morris* (right). Some experimental torpedoes appear in the foreground. (Naval War College Museum.)

The *Wave*. This 82-foot ferryboat, completed in 1892 by the Herreshoff Manufacturing Company of Bristol, transported workers from Government Landing in Newport to the Naval Torpedo Station on Goat Island.

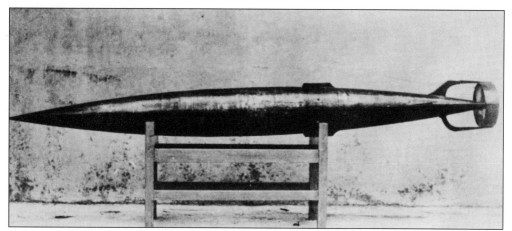

Fish Torpedo. The first torpedo built by the Naval Torpedo Station (in 1871) was of the automobile or "fish" type. Air-driven, it had a range of 200 yards and a speed of 6 to 8 knots. The warhead was composed of 100 pounds of dynamite—a new explosive at that time. (Naval War College Museum.)

Ericsson Torpedo. During the 1870s and 1880s, the Naval Torpedo Station was experimenting with controllable torpedoes like this Ericsson. It was propelled and steered by compressed air fed through an 800-foot rubber hose, which was unreeled as the torpedo ran through the water at 3 knots. (Naval War College Museum.)

1874 – THE FIRST PHOTOGRAPH EVER TAKEN OF AN EXPLOD-
ING TORPEDO (SPAR TYPE) (NEWPORT HARBOR)

Spar Torpedo. At Newport, the Naval Torpedo Station's interest in the Spar Torpedo, used with some success in the Civil War, centered around an electrically detonated modification. The original Spar Torpedo was exploded on contact or by means of a lanyard. The torpedo consisted of an explosive charge fastened to the end of a spar, which was secured to a boat and rigged so that it could be projected forward or abeam and lowered below the waterline of an opposing ship. (*NUSCOPE* file photograph.)

Patrick Torpedo, *c.* 1886. A surface-running torpedo, the Patrick was tested in Newport harbor. (*NUSCOPE* file photograph.)

Hall Steam Torpedo, 1892. This one didn't make it to the fleet. Tests conducted at the Naval Torpedo Station in Newport in 1892 indicated that the Hall Torpedo did not measure up to service standards, and work on it was discontinued. (Naval War College Museum.)

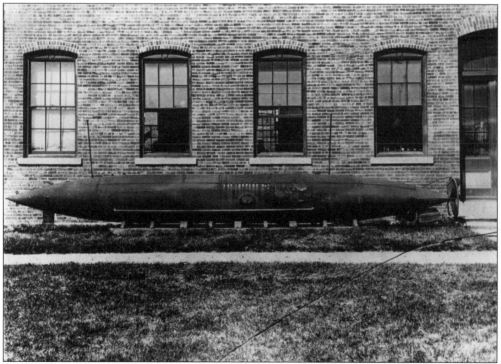

Lay Torpedo, No. 1, 1892. (*NUSCOPE* file photograph.)

Cunningham Rocket Torpedo, 1893. One of several rocket torpedoes evaluated at the Naval Torpedo Station on Goat Island, the Cunningham had its weaknesses. For one thing, its trajectory was unpredictable. Shown here in New Bedford, Massachusetts, this Cunningham torpedo seems to have veered very much off course. (Naval War College Museum.)

Lay-Haight Torpedo. This self-propelled, surface-running torpedo (photographed in March 1894) was driven on the surface by carbonic acid gas carried in a liquid state. It was controlled by an electrical cable from the torpedo. An improved version by George E. Haight was tested at the Naval Torpedo Station in the 1880s. (Naval War College Museum.)

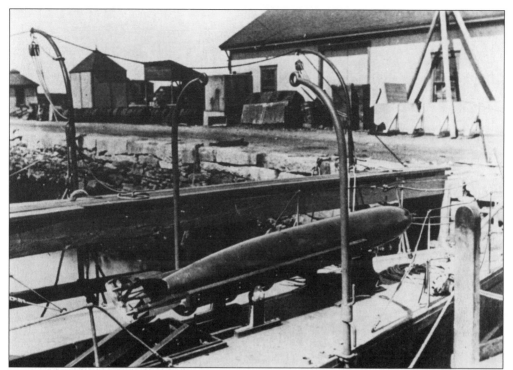

Howell Torpedo, 1896. The last in a series of Howell torpedoes were employed by the first torpedo boat, the USS *Stiletto*, a converted wooden private yacht purchased by the navy and put into service at Newport's Naval Torpedo Station.

USS *Stiletto*. In service from 1887–1911, the *Stiletto* was a former steam yacht converted to an experimental torpedo boat for the navy by a Rhode Island firm, the Herreshoff Manufacturing Company. Its official designation was "Wooden Torpedo Boat-1."

The navy's first torpedo boat, 1889. Originally a private sailing vessel, the *Stiletto* was reconstructed for the navy as a torpedo boat by the Herreshoff Manufacturing Company in Bristol, Rhode Island. (Courtesy *Scientific American*.)

Torpedo boat *Stiletto*. The former yacht, converted to a torpedo boat for the navy, makes a trial torpedo run in the Sakonnet River off Tiverton, Rhode Island.

Firing a Howell Torpedo, *c.* 1890. The torpedo boat *Stiletto* fires a Howell Torpedo from a bow launcher. (Naval War College Museum.)

The *Stiletto*, 1898. Here, the navy's first torpedo boat steams in Narragansett Bay with her full complement on deck.

The *Stiletto* aground in 1889 alongside the Elm Street Pier in Newport, after having been stove in by a steam launch. (*NUSCOPE* file photograph.)

EKLY JOURNAL OF PRACTICAL INFORMATION, ART, SCIENCE, MECHANICS, CHEMISTRY, AND MANUFACTU

LXII.—No. 5.
ESTABLISHED 1845.

NEW YORK, FEBRUARY 1, 1890.

$3.00 A YE
WEEKLY.

NG TORPEDO BOAT NO. 1, UNITED STATES NAVY.

BY LIEUTENANT F. J. DRAKE, U.S.N.

irst sea-going torpedo boat constructed for the States navy was launched from the yard of the off Manufacturing Company, at Bristol, R. I., uary 23. A description of the material of the hull and machinery are composed, and a outline of the internal fittings and armament, e the public at large some idea of the require- which surround the building of a modern sea- orpedo boat having the highest possible speed. pecifications for building this boat were issued Bureau of Ordnance, under whose able direc- present torpedo system of our navy was in- ed and is now being developed into an arm of

our coast defense fully adequate to the demands of the new navy.

The accompanying plate shows plan and longitudi- nal sectional view of hull, and transverse sections at five different points, giving the location of water-tight compartments, boilers, engines, auxiliaries, ejectors, dynamos, launching tubes, and other fittings to be de- scribed.

All material entering into the construction of the hull and machinery was subjected to the standard gov- ernment tests. The frames, shell plating, and all bulk- heads are composed of galvanized steel.

Some important data have been obtained relative to the effect produced upon plates and frames of ten pounds per square foot and under, from galvanizing,

the record of which will be published later i SCIENTIFIC AMERICAN SUPPLEMENT.

The following are the principal dimensions c boat :

Length between perpendiculars	167·5 feet.
Breadth at L. W. plane (moulded)	14·10 "
Breadth extreme	15·05 "
Depth of hold	9·21 "
Draught (ordinary)	4·50 "
Displacement in tons (2,240 pounds)	91·34 "
Tons per inch immersion at L. W. P.	3·02 "
Moment to alter trim one inch at L. W. P.	18·81 foot ton
Area of midship section	42·36 square f
Area of L. W. P.	1297·89
Center of gravity of L. W. P. abaft Section 45	4·94 feet.
Section 45, abaft forward perpendicular or stem	67·5 "

(Continued on page 71.)

Sea-going Torpedo Boat No. 1. The *Cushing*, the navy's first ocean-going torpedo boat, was built by the Herreshoff Manufacturing Company and launched on January 23, 1890. This page from the *Scientific American* details the new experimental vessel. (Courtesy *Scientific American*.)

The *Cushing*, 1890. This drawing shows the navy's new torpedo boat with two torpedo tubes at the bow, located above the water line port and starboard. The deck has three small rapid-fire guns. (Courtesy *Scientific American*.)

The torpedo boat *Cushing* in Newport, 1900. In this turn-of-the-century picture, the *Cushing* sports a new coat of dark-night camouflage paint. (Naval War College Museum.)

War with Spain. In this illustration made during the Spanish-American War, the torpedo boats *Cushing* and *Talbot*, the first (TB-1) and one of the last (TB-15) of their era, join the blockading U.S. fleet off Cuba.

Seaman Apprentice Ernst Fisher Church, USN, of Tiverton, Rhode Island. He attended Moses Brown School in Providence and interrupted his studies to serve under Admiral George Dewey in the Spanish-American War aboard the USS *Olympia* in the battle of Manila. In 1951, his daughter, Frances Church Flynn, a graduate of the Rhode Island School of Design, entered civil service as an engineering draftsman at the Naval Torpedo Station and was one of the first women to hold a top administrative post at Newport, rising to become head of graphic arts at successor navy laboratories in Newport. (*NUSCOPE*.)

USS *Porter*. Trial runs for the *Porter* (TB-6), considerably longer than the *Cushing*, clocked the course at a good 28.6 knots. The TB-6 distinguished itself in the Spanish-American War. The steel-hulled torpedo boat cost $147,000 to build. It was launched in 1896 and served until 1912, when it was struck from the navy roles and sold.

The *Dupont* in Rhode Island waters. Launched in 1897, the *Dupont* (TB-7) went on patrol in Narragansett Bay and saw service in the Spanish-American War.

Capture. This drawing by F. Cressan Schell depicts the heroic capture of an armed Schwartzkopf Torpedo by Ensign Gillis of the *Porter* during the Spanish-American War.

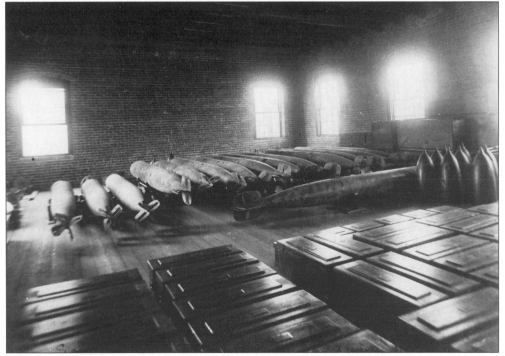

Souvenirs of war, 1900. Captured Schwartzkopf Torpedoes from navy action near Cuba in the Spanish-American war were stored at the Naval Torpedo Station in Newport. (Naval War College Museum.)

The torpedo boat *Dupont* patrolling in Narragansett Bay.

Damage to the *Dupont*.
Following a collision at the
Naval Torpedo Station, navy
inspectors survey the damaged
bow of the USS *Dupont*, one
of the navy's torpedo boats
assigned to Newport. (Courtesy
Scientific American.)

Torpedo practice, 1900. In its issue of March 10, 1900, the *Scientific American* documented torpedo practice launching in Newport waters. The torpedo boat is the *Morris* (TB-14). (Courtesy *Scientific American*.)

Torpedo boat *Morris* (TB-14). Built by the Herreshoff firm of Bristol, Rhode Island, and launched on April 18, 1898, the *Morris* was commissioned at Newport the next month with Lieutenant C.E. Fox in command. The *Morris* was 140 feet long, displaced 105 tons, and carried three 18-inch torpedo tubes.

The crew of the *Morris* preparing a practice launch of a Whitehead Torpedo.

Torpedo firing, 1906. Working out of the Naval Torpedo Station, the torpedo boat *Morris* fires a Whitehead Torpedo in July 1906. This photograph was presented to the Naval Torpedo Station by W.B. Childs. (Naval War College Archives.)

The *Morris* at Newport. The *Morris* has her sun-shielding canvas in place as the torpedo boat stands at pierside at the Naval Torpedo Station. Commissioned in Newport on May 11, 1898, the *Morris* remained at the Naval Torpedo Station until World War I, when she spent time on patrol in the West Indies. Returning to Newport in 1919, the *Morris* was decommissioned but remained active as a range tender for some five years. Struck from the roles, the boat was sold in 1924.

Torpedo training. Crewmen of the *Talbot* (TB-15) ready a torpedo for test firing. The *Talbot* saw service in Cuban waters in the Spanish-American War.

The *Gwin* (TB-16). The *Gwin*, shown fully armed and underway in Narragansett Bay, was a sister ship to the *Talbot* (TB-15).

The USS *Talbot* (TB-15). The *Talbot* was one of twelve steel-hulled, ocean-going torpedo boats—and, with the *Gwin*, one of the two smallest—built for the navy by the Herreshoff firm in Bristol, Rhode Island. (U.S. Naval Historical Center/Naval War College Museum.)

Three
The Naval Training Station and Naval War College

Naval War College, 1884. In 1883, Coasters Harbor Island became navy property, and the following year, the former Newport Alms House building became home to the new Naval War College, the first school of its kind in the world. (Naval War College Museum.)

Commodore Stephen B. Luce, U.S. Naval Academy Class of 1847. Luce founded the Naval Training Station in 1883 in Newport and the Naval War College the next year, in 1884. He also served as the college's first president. (Photograph of painting courtesy of United States Naval Academy, Special Collections and Archives Division, William W. Jeffries Memorial Archives.)

Luce Hall, Naval War College (postcard). The first authorized new construction for the Naval War College, this building was erected in 1892, eight years after the college began in Newport. It was named Luce Hall in 1934 to honor the college founder and first president, Stephen Bleecker Luce. (Naval War College Museum.)

Naval War College classroom scene, 1888. Officer students listen to a lecture on naval tactics in the building that was the original site of the Naval War College at Newport. From 1884 to 1889, the college was located here. Later called "Founders Hall," the building is now the site of the Naval War College Museum. (Naval War College Museum.)

Rear Admiral Alfred Thayer Mahan, president of the Naval War College in Newport, 1886–1889, 1892–1893. The painting by Alexander James hangs in the college conference center in Mahan Hall. (Naval War College Museum.)

Training squadron at Newport, c. 1886. The Newport training fleet was regularly anchored in the harbor area in the 1880s and 1890s. The ships are (from left to right) USS *Jamestown*, USS *Saratoga*, USS *New Hampshire*, and USS *Richmond*. The *New Hampshire*, shown berthed at Coasters Harbor Island, was the principal Naval Training Station ship for fifty-three years, replaced by USS *Constellation* in 1893, four years after the *New Hampshire* had left the Newport scene. (U.S. Naval Historical Center.)

Naval Training Station, c. 1885. This is the earliest known view of the training station established on Coasters Harbor Island in 1883. This U.S. Marine sentry booth is approximately where a small brick building for visitor information and guard staff is today, just inside Gate 1. The large white building is the former Newport Alms House and the place where the Naval War College began in October 1884. (Naval War College Museum.)

Training ship *Monongahela* in Newport. The *Monongahela* was typical of the early sailing vessels used for training purposes by the Naval Training Station in Newport. (Naval War College Museum.)

Crewmen of the *New Hampshire* at drill. Until 1889, the training ship *New Hampshire*, one of the oldest training ships of the American Navy, was stationed at Coasters Harbor Island offshore Newport. It left Newport that year following a severe epidemic among the young men in the training brigades and was replaced by the USS *Constellation* four years later. (Naval War College Museum.)

Swedish gymnastics. At the Naval Training Station, the curriculum called for an hour a day to be devoted to Swedish gymnastics, which were said to develop in the young men "muscular strength, alertness, and power to think and act quickly in any emergency." (Naval War College Museum.)

Boat drill. An important feature of a sailor's training, boat drills were a regular part of the seamanship program at Newport.

Signal School, Newport. Members of the Signal School at the Naval Training Station were selected by examination from volunteer candidates. Instruction was given in wigwag and semaphore signaling, flag hoists, Blinker and Ardois messages, and in radio work. (Naval War College Museum.)

THE YEOMAN SCHOOL

The yeomen are the clerks of the service. One division is trained for attending to correspondence, files, and papers pertaining to matters of military law; the other for keeping the accounts of the service

Yeoman School. The Naval Training Station offered a program for yeomen, the clerks of the service. One division was trained for attending to correspondence, files, and papers pertaining to matters of military law; another was trained in keeping accounts of the service. (Naval War College Museum.)

Naval Training Station class. Seamen at Newport listen to an instructor and consult the references in their geography texts. (Naval War College Museum.)

Marine guard apprentice training, 1889. (Naval War College Museum.)

Seaman Gunners School, Newport, *c.* 1900. (Naval War College Museum.)

Training ships at Newport, *c.* 1900. The *Reine Mercedes*, the *Cumberland*, and the *Constellation* supported the Naval Training Station programs. The *Constellation*, which dated from Revolutionary War times and saw active service into the twentieth century, was often referred to as "the oldest U.S. Navy ship afloat." (Naval War College Museum.)

Four

The Navy in Newport: 1900–1940

The president comes to Newport, 1906. President Theodore Roosevelt arrives for a naval conference in Newport. (Naval War College Museum.)

The *Holland* at Newport. The navy's first successful submarine, the *Holland*, was designed by inventor John P. Holland and built in 1898 by Crescent Shipyards in Elizabeth, New Jersey. It was accepted by the government on April 11, 1900, and commissioned in the navy in October 1900. It had three tubes—one for a Whitehead Torpedo and two for hurling dynamite shells with compressed air—and a gun for armament. The USS *Holland* (designated SS-1 by the navy) was demonstrated and tested in Newport waters by the Naval Torpedo Station. (Newport Historical Society.)

Something new in Newport. By the turn of the century, a new type of vessel—the submarine—was added to the navy's fleet. Beginning in 1875, inventor John P. Holland of Paterson, New Jersey, built six submarines with private funding. He cruised the Passaic River in his first one, a slender cigar-shaped vessel 16 feet long and 2 feet in diameter. In 1893, when Congress appropriated money for experimental submarines, Holland won the competition, but the boat (his seventh, called the *Plunger*) was not completed. The navy's *Holland* (above, c. 1900) was his eighth design. It was tested in Newport. (*NUSCOPE* file photograph.)

U.S. Naval Training Station, Newport, 1906. From left to right are the Naval War College, the administration building, the commandant's quarters, the training ship *Constellation*, and Marine barracks. (*NUSCOPE*.)

Government Landing (postcard).

Naval Torpedo Station, Newport (postcard).

Naval Torpedo Station, Goat Island (postcard, *c.* 1907). The caption on this postcard, printed in Holland, says that the Naval Torpedo Station included "a school maintained by the Government for the experimenting with and maintenance of various explosives. A great number of torpedoes and electrical instruments are stored, and it is here that naval officers go for practice during the summer months." (From enlarged *NUSCOPE* file photograph.)

Torpedo School on Goat Island, *c.* 1907. A torpedo course was started at the Naval Training Station shortly after the station was established. It varied from a few weeks to longer periods and was open to officers and enlisted men. In 1889, the Torpedo School was consolidated on Goat Island with the Naval War College. The schools separated in 1892, when the Naval War College completed construction of its first academic building (now Luce Hall) on Coasters Harbor Island. (Naval War College Museum.)

Naval War College war game class, 1914. Officer students engage in a naval war game as part of their studies at the Naval War College in Newport. War gaming became a formal part of the college curriculum in 1894. (Naval War College Museum.)

World War I navy recruitment poster, 1915. This is one of several well-known pieces by artist Howard Chandler Christy. (Naval War College Museum.)

German submarine at Newport, 1916. When a German submarine, the U-53, came to Narragansett Bay in early October 1916, its commander, Captain Hans Rose of the German Navy, visited the Naval Torpedo Station, the Naval Training Station, and the Naval War College, and exchanged military courtesies with senior officers at those commands. The U-boat, with its tall radio antenna masts along the vessel's sides, was photographed on October 7, 1916, with its national and naval flags unfurled. In the background is USS *Birmingham*. Some hours after departing, the U-53 attacked Allied (but not American) shipping near Nantucket Lightship, and the survivors were brought to Newport.

U.S. Naval Training Station, 1917. This is a typical drill formation on Dewey Field, Coasters Harbor Island, during the First World War, when over 75,000 personnel were trained at Newport. It was during this period that the station expanded beyond Coasters Harbor Island to include Coddington Point to the north. Ships shown are the USS *Constellation* and USS *Boxer*. (Naval War College Museum.)

Same scene, late fall or winter 1917–18. Note the wartime tent quarters on the mainland in the background of both pictures. (Naval War College Museum.)

Barracks B, c. 1910. Built in 1900, this was the first quarters facility constructed at the Naval Training Center. It contained a large drill hall and a mess hall. The building served the station through World War I and World War II, but was destroyed by fire in 1946. The ship masts in the background belong to the USS *Constellation*, which was moored next to the building from 1907–12. (Naval War College Museum.)

Building 70, Research and Blueprint Shop. This two-story building cost $29,890 when it was built for the Naval Torpedo Station in 1917. (1946 photograph, Naval War College Archives.)

Building 72, Chemical and Metallurgical Laboratory, built in 1918 at a cost of $35,000. (1945 photograph, Naval War College Archives.)

Newport, 1918. Navy personnel keep things in order as a truck tows field pieces to the polo grounds in this photograph taken on a downtown Newport street on August 6, 1918.

Hospital Corps School, 1918. The World War Hospital Corps Training School was part of the Naval Training Station at Newport. Upon graduation, corpsmen received a hospital apprentice first class rating with pay of $38.40 per month, plus allowances. (*Newport Navalog.*)

Naval Communication Station, 1918. Construction was just getting underway in this scene on Coasters Harbor Island near the Naval War College and Training Station buildings. Established on August 14, 1903, the Naval Communication Station at Newport served through two world wars and later had the distinction of being the navy's oldest active communication station. (*Newport Navalog.*)

Naval Torpedo Station, December 1920. The station on Goat Island witnessed considerable expansion of its buildings and facilities throughout the war, with much of the small island's space occupied as the postwar period began. (*NUSCOPE* file photograph.)

Aerial view of Goat Island in about the same period. The Naval War College and Naval Training Station can be seen in the upper left. (*NUSCOPE* file photograph.)

Naval Training Station, 1923. A formation on Dewey Field, Coasters Harbor Island, spells out "Newport." The buildings in the background are, from left to right, the Naval War College (now Luce Hall of the enlarged college complex), the Naval Communications Station (built in 1917), and the Naval Training Station administration building. (Naval War College Museum.)

Torpedo plane of the early 1920s. A twin-float bomber torpedo plane, an SC-1, releases its torpedo. The navy's first test drop occurred in 1917, and the navy commissioned the first torpedo squadron in 1920. Three decades later, in World War II, navy and marine aircraft sank more than six hundred enemy ships in the Pacific Theater. (Naval War College Museum.)

Seaplane launch in the Newport harbor, 1928. The first two torpedo planes (PT-1s) were assigned to the Naval Torpedo Station in 1921. During the 1920s, the Newport station became more and more involved in modifying Mark 7 Torpedoes for aircraft use and evaluating new torpedo aircraft. New and larger torpedoes were developed in the 1930s. (Naval War College Museum.)

Training station headquarters, c. 1925. In 1914, the former Newport Alms House and site of the original Naval War College became headquarters of the Naval Training Station, established on Coasters Harbor Island in 1883. Recruit training continued in Newport until 1951, when a Newport Naval Station Command was formed and continued to use the building for administrative purposes. In 1961, the Newport Naval Base, established in the Second World War with responsibility for the total naval presence in Narragansett Bay, also used the building as headquarters. The base and station were disestablished in 1973, and the building reverted to the Naval War College. (Naval War College Museum.)

Goat Island, c. 1930. Beyond the Naval Torpedo Station on Goat Island (in the center), the small island in the background is Rose Island. At the top is Conanicut Island (Jamestown), with the West Passage of Narragansett Bay and part of the western Rhode Island mainland in the distance.

Naval Torpedo Station, Newport, 1934. This view of Goat Island, looking south, was photographed by the public works department in April 1934 to show the progress of work on a new bulkhead near the piers.

Naval Torpedo Station, Newport, 1937. This public works department photograph, taken in mid-winter at Goat Island, shows the progress of work on a platform for a new ferry landing for the station.

Quonset Point Naval Air Station (NAS). Located on the west shore of Narragansett Bay, the Quonset Point NAS, North Kingstown, was commissioned in July 1940 as part of the general military needs buildup of the U.S. Naval Operating Base, which was established earlier that year with headquarters in Newport. (Naval War College Museum.)

Officers quarters on the south end of Goat Island. (Naval War College Archives.)

President Franklin Delano Roosevelt visiting Newport, 1940. As World War II intensified in Europe in 1940, Washington approved measures for military needs, including the increased recruitment of naval personnel. President Roosevelt was particularly interested in naval training and visited the Newport Naval Training Station in September 1940. (Naval War College Museum.)

Five

The Navy in Newport in World War II

Naval Torpedo Station, 1940. As World War II raged in Europe, the navy weapons activity on Goat Island, Newport, grew enormously—in buildings and staff—since its establishment in 1869 as the country's first experimental torpedo station. Newport's waterfront piers and downtown business section can be seen in the near background. The vista stretches to adjacent Middletown and the Sakonnet River (at the top), which provided a direct seaway connection to Long Island Sound for the textile mills of Fall River, Massachusetts, in their heyday. (*NUSCOPE* file photograph.)

The USS *Constellation* in the Second World War. Recruits stand in formation at Constellation Point. Dewey Field and the Naval Training Station building (now Luce Hall of the Naval War College) make up the background to the left of the training ship. (Naval War College Museum.)

Naval Training Station Barracks at Coddington Point. As America found itself engulfed in war, Newport—like so many other parts of the land—gave its all to the nation's effort. Almost overnight, these barracks went up in a formerly sparsely used area near the Naval Training Station on Coasters Harbor Island. The wooden barracks were typical of the new recruit quarters. Most of these buildings lasted well after the war ended in 1945. (Naval War College Museum.)

Exercising with rifles, Kidd Field, 1941. (Naval War College Museum.)

Exercising with music: outdoor calisthenics for the navy recruits in 1941. (Naval War College Museum.)

Coddington Point, 1942. By the time of this photograph (taken August 5, 1942), the U.S. Naval Training Station had pretty much taken over Coddington Point. (Naval War College Archives.)

Coddington Point, 1943. By the second year of the war, navy recruitment and training were in full swing at Newport, and navy housing covered practically all of Coddington Point, as shown in this photograph taken on April 15, 1943. (Naval War College Archives.)

Navy housing. Those famous Quonset huts went up in Newport, too, as the navy found a less expensive way to provide housing for the ever-increasing flow of service recruits. (Naval War College Museum.)

New recruits, 1942. Recruits march in drill formation at Kidd Field, Coddington Point, in the early days of America's participation in the war. (Naval War College Museum.)

Coddington Cove, 1941. Newport's airport at Coddington Cove was in a rural area that would witness large-scale use by the navy during the war for facilities and training. (Naval War College Museum.)

Coddington Cove, 1943. The U.S. Naval Supply Depot was photographed on July 3, 1943. (Naval War College Archives.)

Barracks B, Naval Training Station. The first and largest of the government recruiting quarters at the Naval Training Station, this complex served in two world wars. With the building destroyed by fire just after the finish of World War II, the site was later occupied by three Naval War College buildings: Spruance Hall, Conolly Hall, and Hewitt Hall (see Chapter Six). (Naval War College Museum.)

Barracks C, a recruit battalion facility of three interconnected buildings, built in 1904. It remained the property of the Naval Training Station until 1946, when it was taken over by the Naval War College. Today called Sims Hall, it is home to the college's war gaming department. The view above is of the buildings in 1945, during the Second World War. (Naval War College Museum.)

Building boom, 1944. Military construction was an ongoing thing for the nation at war—and for the navy in Newport—as this scene attests. (Naval War College Archives.)

Naval Torpedo Station magazine, 1942. Throughout the naval complex on Goat Island and elsewhere, magazines and other storage facilities sprang up in wartime Newport. (Naval War College Archives.)

Prudence Island, 1942. The navy used this small offshore island and other nearby sites in Narragansett Bay for naval magazines to store explosives during the war. (Naval War College Archives.)

Naval Torpedo Station munitions storage and sheds. (Naval War College Archives.)

Building 73, a garage, 1945. (Naval War College Archives.)

Building 94, an assembly building, built in 1940. Additions were later constructed to give this structure three stories. (Naval War College Archives.)

Building 96, a facility for manufacturing explosives, built in 1941. (Naval War College Archives.)

Building 98, an administration building, built in 1941–1942. (Naval War College Archives.)

Naval Torpedo Station on Goat Island in September 1943. (*NUSCOPE* file photograph.)

Gould Island, 1942. As every aspect of the Naval Torpedo Station's activities were undergoing rapid wartime expansion, buildings were constructed and functions relocated from the main production facility on Goat Island to various points within the Narragansett Bay area. A major site was Gould Island, used for aerial torpedo testing, torpedo test firing, aircraft range support, and housing a torpedo factory overhaul shop. (*NUSCOPE* file photograph.)

Gould Island, 1944. In this close-up of the firing pier at the north end of Gould Island, the camera has caught an exercise torpedo at the moment of its launch into the waters of Narragansett Bay. (Naval War College Museum.)

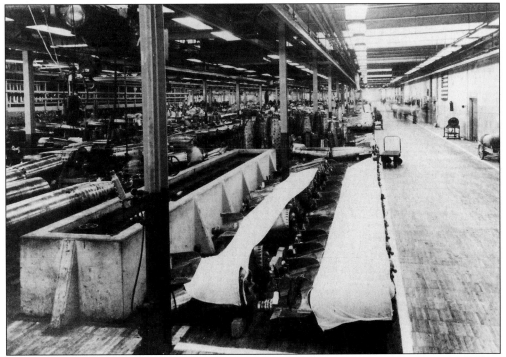

Gould Island, 1944. A Naval Torpedo Station facility, this torpedo factory overhaul shop operated on Gould Island during World War II. (Naval War College Museum.)

Gould Island, February 9, 1944, showing aviation improvement at the island's southern tip. (Naval War College Archives.)

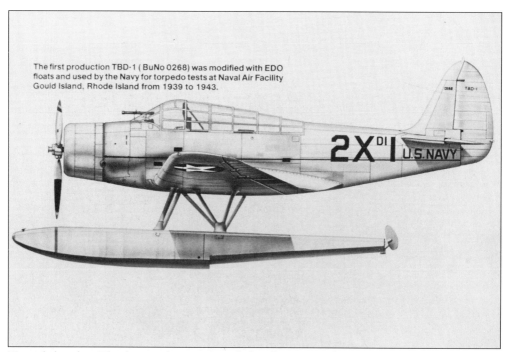

The first production TBD-1 (BuNo 0268) was modified with EDO floats and used by the Navy for torpedo tests at Naval Air Facility Gould Island, Rhode Island from 1939 to 1943.

Torpedo bomber. The first production torpedo bomber was modified with floats and used by the navy for torpedo tests at Gould Island from 1939 to 1943.

Patrol Torpedo (PT) boat. The development of the self-propelled torpedo, along with the advent of World War II and the heavy loss of ships at Pearl Harbor, created the need for a swift, highly maneuverable boat which could be quickly and inexpensively produced to deliver the weapon against the enemy ships. The PT boats were to have more hours of actual combat in the war than any other navy ship. During the war, the PT squadrons trained at Melville Point in Portsmouth, Rhode Island, part of the U.S. Naval Operating Base at Newport. In the picture above, an early PT boat (c. 1942) fires a Mark 13 Torpedo on a training run.

MTBSTC insignia. The Motor Torpedo Boat Squadrons Training Center at Melville, Rhode Island, prepared officers and men for the PT boat squadrons of the navy in World War II. It was here that John Fitzgerald Kennedy trained prior to his assignment to the Western Pacific Theater during the war. His experiences became the subject of a book and the Warner Brothers motion picture *PT-109* starring Cliff Robertson as the later president.

Melville Point, April 13, 1943. Home to PT boat training, Melville Point has a long history of involvement with the military. At the outset of the Civil War, Melville was a tree-shaded private summer resort that became the location of Lowell General Hospital. Wounded Union and Confederate soldiers arrived there by boat, and during the three years of the hospital's operation, more than ten thousand were treated. After the war, the site reverted to private ownership, with part of it later becoming a navy fuel depot, the Bradford Coaling Station. In World War II, because of the adjacent fuel depot and the short distance to Newport and the Naval Torpedo Station, Melville Point again came into military use as the nation's only training center for the "Mosquito Fleet." The natural lagoon was dredged, an outlet channel improved, and a community of 286 buildings, mostly Quonsets, arose beside it. (Naval War College Archives.)

PT boat training center. PT boat training was conducted at this site in Melville, Rhode Island, seven miles north of Newport on Aquidneck Island. In the summer of 1943, at the height of operations, the Motor Torpedo Boat Squadrons Training Center housed seventeen hundred men. (Naval War College Museum.)

PT boat training at Melville. When the training center closed in October 1945, it had graduated 2,017 officers and 12,500 enlisted men. This was an elite, all-volunteer group who, unlike other military units at high risk, received no additional "hazardous duty" pay. (Naval War College Museum.)

John F. Kennedy's class at the PT boat training center, October 1942. John Fitzgerald Kennedy (rear row, seventh from right) trained at Melville and served with PT squadrons 2 and 5 in the Pacific Theater. While on PT-109 west of New Georgia, his boat was rammed on August 2, 1943. Kennedy's navy service was the subject of the motion picture *PT-109* starring Cliff Robertson as the young navy lieutenant. Kennedy received the Purple Heart and also the navy and marine corps medals. In 1961, he became the 35th president of the United States. (John F. Kennedy Library, Boston.)

President Kennedy and Cliff Robertson in the Oval Office on April 24, 1963. The actor was the president's personal choice for the role of the young Kennedy as a navy lieutenant in *PT-109*. (John F. Kennedy Library, Boston.)

Cliff Robertson in *PT-109*. This 1963 Warner Brothers' film presents the story of Lieutenant (j.g.) John F. Kennedy in command of his first vessel, one of the navy's patrol torpedo boats assigned to harass the enemy in the Solomon Islands. Young Kennedy, portrayed in the film by Robertson (who later won an Oscar for *Charly*), trained at the Motor Torpedo Boat Squadrons Training Center in Melville, Rhode Island, then part of the U.S. Naval Operating Base at Newport. Kennedy's training and Melville are mentioned several times in the course of the movie. In addition to Robertson, the cast included two young actors later to find popular roles in TV series, Robert Culp and Robert Blake. (Warner Brothers.)

Naval mine and net depot, Melville, 1943. This facility, also at Melville Point, worked on harbor defense nets for protection against enemy submarines. (Naval War College Archives.)

The Naval Base Inshore Patrol at Long Wharf in downtown Newport. (Naval War College Museum.)

Kate Smith at Newport. The well-known singer visited Newport as a USO performer in 1943. Shown with her are Admiral William S. Pye, president of the Naval War College, and Captain C.W. McGrudder, commanding officer of the station. (Naval War College Museum.)

Hammersmith Farm welcomes the navy. The Auchincloss' Hammersmith Farm on Newport's Ocean Drive hosted Newport's navy recruits during the war. Years later, Hammersmith Farm would be the site of the John Kennedy-Jacqueline Bouvier wedding reception. (Naval War College Museum.)

Navy WAVES being briefed at Newport. (Naval War College Archives.)

Coasters Harbor Island in wartime. The Naval War College and Naval Training Station buildings can be seen in the left foreground of this March 1944 photograph, and the sprawling training station barracks and other facilities fill the center portion at Coddington Point. (Naval War College Museum.)

Six
Postwar Consolidation and Change

Admiral Raymond A. Spruance, president of the Naval War College from March 1946 to June 1948. At the end of World War II, Admiral Spruance was named commander-in-chief of the Pacific, replacing Chester Nimitz, who became Chief of Naval Operations. Spruance served in his new position only ten months and joined the Naval War College as president on March 1, 1946. It is said that Spruance elected to go to Newport because he always considered the college presidency as one of the most important jobs in the navy. He knew the Newport institution from personal experience, having graduated from the college's Senior Course in 1927 and serving two separate times on the staff in the next decade. As president, Spruance revitalized the school from the short course specialized training facility it had become during the war and introduced a new and challenging curriculum. (Courtesy Naval War College Public Affairs Office.)

Spruance Hall. Work on the first building of a new complex at the Naval War College began in the summer of 1970 during the administration of Vice Admiral Richard G. Colbert as NWC president. The view above shows the entrance to Spruance and Conolly Halls. Spruance Hall (to the left) contains Spruance Auditorium, the college's largest such facility. (Darcy Associates, Ltd.)

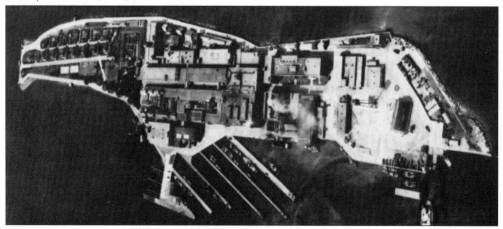

Naval Torpedo Station, 1945. Within six years of the end of World War II, the historic station established in Newport in 1869 would be permanently disestablished, with the experimental and research work spun off into successor organizations and the manufacture of torpedoes given over to private industry. Navy buildings on Goat Island were razed in 1952 after the Naval Torpedo Station closed. (Naval War College Archives.)

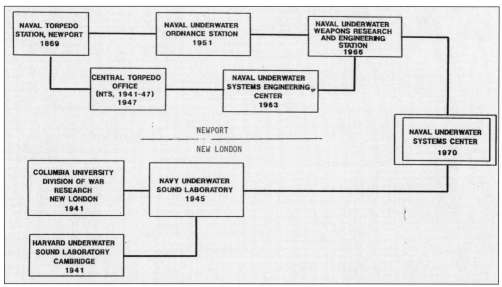

Naval Torpedo Station genealogy. After the war, a number of changes took place in naval education and training at Newport, as well as in the research and development area that grew out of the pioneer Naval Torpedo Station (1869–1951). In 1970, the Naval Underwater Systems Center was established, merging the Newport line with the Navy Underwater Sound Laboratory in nearby Connecticut, which had conducted wartime sonar and acoustics research. (Adapted from *Meeting the Submarine Challenge* by John Merrill and Lionel D. Wyld.)

Central Torpedo Office, Newport, 1961. Established in 1941 within the Naval Torpedo Station on Goat Island, the Central Torpedo Office began the transition of torpedo manufacture to private industry. Displayed in front of the building is the so-called "auto-mobile" or Fish Torpedo, the first torpedo built by the Newport station. Air-driven, it had a range of 200 yards and a speed of 6 to 8 knots. The warhead charge was 100 pounds of dynamite, a new explosive at that time. (U.S. Navy photograph by B. Martel, CTO Photographic Branch.)

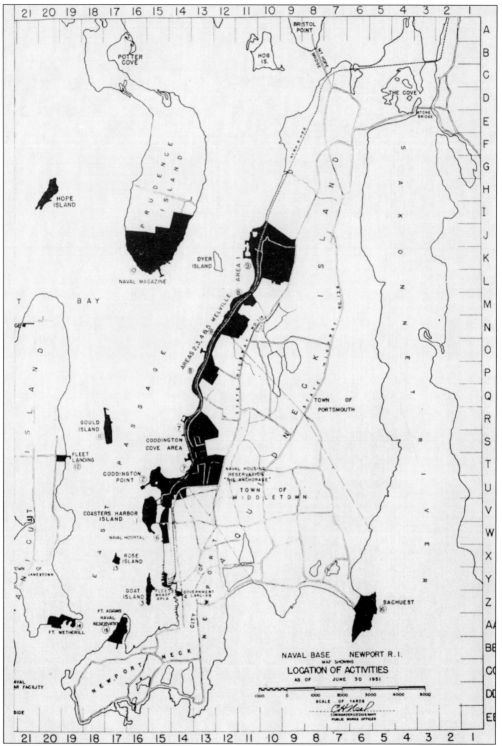

U.S. Naval Base at Newport, 1951. The location of each of the component naval activities comprising the naval base is highlighted in this Naval Base Public Works illustration.

Naval Underwater Ordnance Station display, SERVICE FOR SEAPOWER, in a downtown Newport storefront locale. The Naval Underwater Ordnance Station (1951–1966) served as a bridge from the disestablishment of the Naval Torpedo Station to the establishment of the Naval Underwater Weapons Research and Engineering Station in 1966. (Naval War College Archives.)

A hurricane sweeping across the ordnance station, 1954. The Naval Underwater Ordnance Station was heavily hit by Hurricane Carol, and the flooding engulfed a number of cars in this NUOS parking lot.

A hurricane hits Newport, 1954. Hurricane Carol wreaked havoc at the naval base and throughout the Newport area in August 1954. (Naval War College Archives.)

Hurricane Carol in Newport. At Newport's Long Wharf, the navy's diving operations try to assess damage caused by the hurricane in the Midway Landing area. (Naval War College Archives.)

Fort Adams, 1953. From the time the navy planned to use it as midshipmen's quarters for a relocated U.S. Naval Academy during the Civil War to the present day, the historic army fort area guarding the harbor entrance has been used for a variety of major maritime events in Newport, including America's Cup and other sailing programs and also for navy recreation and housing. Today, a naval reservation with housing and recreation areas occupies the west shore, abutting Fort Adams State Park and the fort. (Naval War College Archives.)

Summer White House, 1957. President Dwight D. Eisenhower and his family occupied this house in "Senior Officer Country" at the Naval War College complex for their month-long residence in Newport. In 1957, 1958, and 1960, the vacationing president also used Founders Hall (just up the driveway from the house) as his staff headquarters, maintaining an office on the first floor of the original Naval War College building. (Naval War College Archives.)

Student visitors. Pupils from elementary and secondary schools in Newport and nearby towns visit the naval research and scientific facilities as part of the navy's ongoing public affairs and community service programs. Among the participants in the 1960s were these students from two Rhode Island high schools who toured the Naval Underwater Weapons and Engineering Center in Newport. At the top, Cumberland High School students meet with mathematician Joseph R. Babiec (also a resident of that northeast Rhode Island town) in November 1965. In the lower photograph, mathematician Thomas Conrad discusses the center's computer facilities with Bristol High School students in February 1966. (U.S. Navy photographs by A. Boivan and W. Howard.)

Coddington Cove, 1966. The Naval Underwater Weapons Research and Engineering Station (NUWS) was formed in 1966 by combining two navy establishments—the Naval Underwater Systems Engineering Center that grew out of the Central Torpedo Office and the Naval Underwater Ordnance Station that had evolved from the original Naval Torpedo Station. (U.S. Navy/NUWS.)

Navy piers in 1967. The two piers at Coddington Cove are filled with Atlantic Fleet ships. The Cruiser-Destroyer Force was headquartered in Newport and brought nearly sixty ships for homeporting. (U.S. Navy/NUWS.)

From army to navy. The Naval Underwater Weapons Research and Engineering Station at Newport obtained this coastal cargo ship from the U.S. Army for use in torpedo launchings and oceanographic research. Besides its laboratory facilities, the ship could accommodate forty passengers and crew, as well as 859 tons of cargo. (NUWS Centennial Commemoration brochure, 1969.)

USS *Dolphin* at Newport, 1969. An experimental submarine built in 1965, the *Dolphin* (shown in the stillwater basin in Coddington Cove) was used in connection with various deep-sensing and other navy research programs at Newport and at Woods Hole Oceanographic Laboratory near Cape Cod in Massachusetts. (U.S. Navy photograph by G.A. Saad.)

NUSC Headquarters, Newport. The Naval Underwater Systems Center (NUSC) was formed in 1970 by a merger of the Naval Underwater Weapons Research and Engineering Station at Newport and the Navy Underwater Sound Laboratory in New London, Connecticut, as part of the navy laboratory system under the Naval Material Command.

Naval Underwater Systems Center, Newport, c. 1970.

Naval Underwater Systems Center, New London, c. 1970.

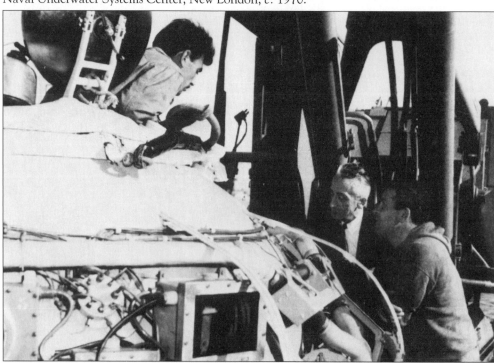

Underwater research. Navy Underwater Sound Laboratory (USL) scientists confer with oceanographer Jacques Cousteau before a research dive. In 1970, USL, which began as a World War II activity involved in sonar and associated acoustics research, became the New London Laboratory of the Naval Underwater Systems Center, with headquarters in Newport.

Oceanographic research. The largest transducer element built in its day, this 15-ton sound source was part of a facility at Eleuthera recovered in July 1972 under the direction of the Naval Underwater Systems Center. It was found to be still operable after six years on the ocean floor. Recording and analysis of data from the Bendix-built piece of equipment were conducted at the Newport center's Bermuda and New London laboratories. (Released photograph, *Journal of Naval Science.*)

Oceanographic research. To understand and predict variability in the upper ocean, navy scientists from Newport and New London participated in projects conducted jointly by laboratories from several NATO nations. This research involved synoptic oceanographic observations around the French-manned Bouèe Laboratoire near the Gulf of Lyons in the Mediterranean. (Released photograph, *Journal of Naval Science.*)

NUSC Headquarters, Newport, 1974. When the navy's Cruiser-Destroyer Force, the Atlantic Fleet, was transferred from Newport to Norfolk, this building was ceded to the Naval Underwater Systems Center and became the entrance for visitors to the Center headquarters and the Newport laboratory. (*NUSCOPE* file photograph.)

NUSC detachment at Seneca Lake, 1974. Newport's Naval Underwater Systems Center maintained an acoustic measurement facility at Seneca Lake in upstate New York. The measurement platform shown above provided support for cranes. These cranes had the capacity to hold 200 tons from which large transducer arrays could be suspended.

Tudor Hill Detachment, Bermuda. Newport's Naval Underwater Systems Center operated this detachment for nearly twenty years and conducted programs in ocean acoustics, electromagnetics, and environmental engineering. The Tudor Hill Detachment was disestablished in 1989.

R/V Erline. The research vessel *R/V Erline* (shown here in October 1974) was a major support craft for the Naval Underwater System Center's Tudor Hill Detachment. It carried out various at-sea programs in the Bermuda area. (U.S. Navy photograph by P. Misisco/NUSC.)

NUSC range in the Bahamas, 1976. Newport's Naval Underwater Systems Center operated the Atlantic Undersea Test and Evaluation Center (AUTEC) located in the Bahamas. AUTEC was a joint project agreement between the United States and the United Kingdom, with the concurrence of the Bahamian government. The flags of all three countries are flown over base headquarters.

A visit to AUTEC. His Excellency British High Commissioner Peter Minnell is met upon arrival in February 1975 for a visit to the Atlantic Undersea Test and Evaluation Center by Commander Bruce Nicholls, Royal Navy liaison officer assigned to AUTEC. (Released photograph, *Journal of Naval Science*.)

Helicopter torpedo retrieval at AUTEC, c.1974. Seconds after the retrieval of an exercise torpedo, this weapon recovery cage and its cargo are en route to the land station. Developed at Newport, this diverless system avoided the use of divers and the attendant risk to personnel during exercise. (Released photograph, *Journal of Naval Science*.)

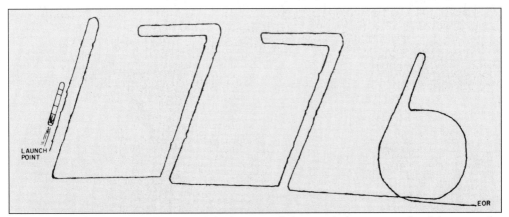

Bicentennial doings at AUTEC, 1976. As part of America's bicentennial celebration, the numerals "1776" were traced on Bahamian waters at an AUTEC range. Coincidentally, it was the navy's 1,976th preparation of a target Mark 27 on the East Coast. The trace above is an exact representation of the actual target track. (*NUSCOPE*.)

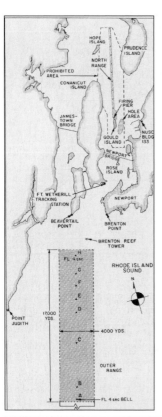

Newport Range. The range complex known as the Newport Range is an underwater tracking and sound-measurement range located in Narragansett Bay. It supports the navy's research and development work.

Range support. Several range craft of the Naval Underwater Systems Center maintain formation as they head toward the entrance to Narragansett Bay in this scene in the early 1970s. Three NUSC exercise-torpedo retriever boats, a YF, and other small support vessels pass under the Newport Bridge as they head south in the East Passage. In the background can be seen Jamestown and Conanicut Island.

Gould Island, 1973. Used extensively in World War II by the Naval Torpedo Station, the island afterwards continued to be used by the station's successors as part of the Newport Range.

Fort Wetherill tracking station, part of the Newport Range, 1973. (U.S. Navy photograph by A.F. Boivan/NUSC.)

Navy drone, 1973. The Naval Underwater Systems Center conducted an experimental program with remote-piloted vehicles (RPVs), which are used in reconnaissance, to adapt them for landing on a ship's deck. (U.S. Navy photograph by A.F. Boivan/NUSC.)

Experimental submarine model, 1973. A proposed configuration, this triple-fin experimental model was fabricated by Newport's Naval Underwater Systems Center with the assistance of Davidson Laboratory of the Stevens Institute of Technology. Dubbed the *Tri-Fin*, it was also called "The Yellow Submarine" due to its coat of bright yellow paint—or, perhaps, because of the popularity of the Beatles' song and movie of the same name. (U.S. Navy photograph by W.S. Howard.)

Navy "firsts" at OCS Newport, 1973. For the first time in the 22-year history of the Officer Candidate School at Newport, a woman—Captain Fran McKee, commanding officer of the Naval Security Group Activity at Fort George G. Meade, Maryland—was principal speaker at graduation ceremonies at the Naval Officer Training Center. It was also the first co-ed OCS class. (*Newport Navalog.*)

Consolidation at Newport, 1974. April 1, 1974, marked the beginning of the Naval Shore Establishment Realignment begun in 1973, as the Newport Naval Base, the Newport Naval Station, and the Naval Officer Training Center were disestablished. The official program for the consolidation ceremonies that formed the Naval Education and Training Center (NETC) was designed by Anthony Sarro, Naval War College graphic arts chief, and depicts the three commands that merged to form NETC. (*Newport Navalog.*)

South gate, Naval Education and Training Center, Coddington Cove. (Photograph by the author.)

Newport: Training Country. This sign at Coddington Cove informs military guests and civilian visitors of some of the affiliated schools and programs in place at the Naval Education and Training Center established at Newport in 1974. The center, along with the prestigious Naval War College, dating from 1884, has given the Newport naval complex the title of "Campus of the Navy." (Darcy Associates, Ltd.)

Navy nurses, 1974. Nurses enrolled at the Officer Indoctrination School at the Naval Education and Training Center try out their dress uniforms for the first and only time during their stay at Newport. At OIS, while learning about being a naval officer, the enrollees wear regular service uniforms. (NETC photograph by JO3 D. Hoch.)

Naval hospital, Newport. The navy acquired a 15-acre site on the mainland for a naval hospital in 1909, and construction began in 1913. The main entrance (shown above) faces westward toward Coasters Harbor Island and the Naval War College. (Darcy Associates, Ltd.)

Naval Chaplains School. Located on Coasters Harbor Island, the chaplains school conducts various courses ranging from one to thirty-nine weeks duration, including the basic course given for newly commissioned chaplains. Started in World War II and disestablished after the war, the Naval Chaplains School was reconvened in Newport in 1951 when the Korean War dictated a need for more clergymen. (Darcy Associates, Ltd.)

Newport Naval Base Seabee. When the Naval Operating Base with headquarters in Newport was established in 1941 to coordinate naval activities in the region, the Naval Air Station at Quonset Point was commissioned on the west shore of Narragansett Bay, and the Naval Construction Battalion Center was established at nearby Davisville. The Seabees were credited with accomplishing an array of wartime tasks, from building bridges and airstrips to construction work for countless facilities needed in the widespread theaters of operation. Their logo (above, in Newport) is a formidable and industrious Seabee carrying tools of his trade and a machine gun for good measure in combat situations. Four decades after the war ended, the Seabees were reestablished by the Secretary of the Navy on July 1, 1985. At Newport, Construction Battalion Unit 408 augments the Naval Mobile Construction Battalion and trains members in construction and military skills. (Photograph by the author.)

Recruiting in Newport. Another of Harold C. Christy's World War I era navy recruiting posters (see chapter five) was reproduced in an issue of *Newport Navalog*, updated with a message for peacetime re-enlistees of the 1970s.

Tennis and the navy. Coach Margaret P. Brummer shows Shirley Hitt how to "shake hands with the racket" in this 1974 *NUSCOPE* photograph (both women were employees at the Naval Underwater Systems Center). Brummer, a graduate of the Tennis America University and certified member of the U.S. Professional Tennis, U.S. Lawn Tennis, U.S. Umpires, and U.S. Professional Tennis Umpires Associations, had a forty-year career in the graphics arts division at Newport. Pat (as she was known widely in tennis circles) became the first umpire nominated to the Tennis Hall of Fame in Newport.

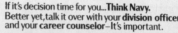

If it's decision time for you...**Think Navy.** Better yet, talk it over with your **division officer** and your **career counselor**–It's important. **STAY NAVY**

Technology transfer conference, 1974. Connecticut Senator A.A. Ribicoff (shown with Naval Underwater Systems Center Technical Director W.L. Clearwaters and Commanding Officer Captain M.C. McFarland) gave the keynote address at a meeting conducted in New London in May 1974. Part of the navy's effort to make its technology resources available for public benefit, the Technology Transfer Seminar was one of the first in the nation devoted to searching for ways in which military-based technical resources could be applied to the solution of domestic and industrial problems. Representatives from educational institutions, industry, navy and other federal agencies, both state and local governments, were brought together to consider the application of Center technology resources to the solution of nonmilitary problems, including those in the areas of ocean resources, transportation, public safety, law enforcement, environment, and urban design. (*NUSCOPE*)

Pier II, 1974. The former site of the headquarters of the Cruiser-Destroyer Force, Atlantic Fleet, this deserted pier at Coddington Cove graphically reflects the navy's decision to transfer the ships and headquarters from Newport to Norfolk, Virginia, in 1973. (U.S. Navy photograph by R.J. Valentine/NUSC.)

Reserve Destroyer Squadron ships at Newport. With the transfer of the Atlantic Fleet ships to Norfolk, the Newport piers were strangely inactive for the first time since the 1950s. In late 1974, Pier I welcomed a number of Reserve Destroyer Squadron vessels and school ships providing support to the Surface Warfare Officers School. Pier II (background, far right), with its now idle fleet headquarters building, began to see occasional support barges for personnel, machine and carpentry shops, etc., and the beginnings of the Shore Intermediate Maintenance Activity (SIMA). (Photograph by the author.)

Katy Field. This recreation park on Coasters Harbor Island was named for the sloop *Katy*, which in 1775 became the first ship of the Rhode Island Navy and later, as the USS *Providence*, was one of the first five ships of the Continental Navy and the first command of John Paul Jones. (See chapter one.) The site was dedicated on the occasion of the national bicentennial on July 4, 1976, at the Naval Education and Training Center in Newport. (Photograph by the author.)

Naval War College Museum, 1978. The Naval War College celebrated the return to its first home in 1974 by naming the building Founders Hall. Two years later, planning began for making the building the site of a college museum, and in May 1978, the museum opened on the first floor, featuring exhibits on the history of naval warfare and the naval heritage of Narragansett Bay. Additional renovations took place during 1983–1984, and the museum opened in November 1984 with exhibits on its two main floors, administrative offices on the third floor, a finished basement, and a rear annex with elevator and stairways. (Naval War College Museum.)

Founders Hall: National Historic Landmark. The original building of the Naval War College, which became the home of the Naval War College Museum in the 1970s, was declared a Registered National Historic Landmark in 1965. (Photograph by the author.)

Mark 48 Torpedo display, 1977. At Newport's Naval Underwater Systems Center, an exercise torpedo of the inservice Mark 48 Torpedo line is compared with the Naval Torpedo Station's Fish Torpedo of a century earlier. (U.S. Navy photograph by G.A. Saad.)

Submarine construction, 1979. The navy's ballistic missile submarine USS *Michigan* (SSBN 727) is under construction at the Electric Boat Division of General Dynamics in Groton, Connecticut. In the foreground are ships of the U.S. Coast Guard at the Coast Guard pier at the NUSC New London Laboratory. (Naval Underwater Systems Center, New London Laboratory Photographic Division.)

Naval Underwater Systems Center, Newport. This panoramic aerial of the Center in the 1980s looks southward to Newport Beach (known locally as First Beach) and the open water of Long Island Sound. (U.S. Navy photograph by L. Mongeon.)

Seven
Epilogue

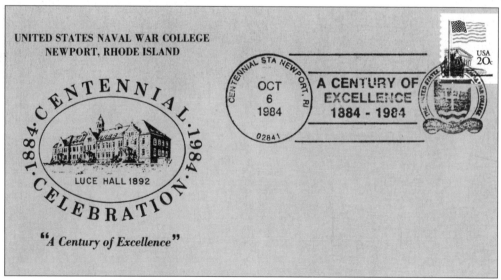

"A Century of Excellence." In 1984, the U.S. Naval War College issued a special philatelic cover in connection with its centennial celebration. The cachet, in oval design, depicts Luce Hall (1892), the first authorized new construction for the college. A special postmark was available at the designated Centennial Station in Newport, with a cancellation bearing the Naval War College crest and the words: "A Century of Excellence 1884–1984." (Author's collection.)

U.S. Naval War College today (postcard). As the nation's oldest service college, officers of all United States armed forces and of the navies of many foreign countries are provided with postgraduate studies to prepare them for career challenges. (Naval War College Museum.)

Founders Hall, Naval War College. The original building of the Naval War College, Founders Hall was built by the city of Newport in 1820 for use as a poorhouse. Designated a National Historical Landmark, it was placed on the Register of Historic Sites in 1964. It was here that the Naval War College, the first of its kind in the world, began in 1884, and Admiral Alfred Thayer Mahan wrote his classic treatise on *The Influence of Sea Power Upon History*, published in 1890. Founders Hall is now the home of the Naval War College Museum. (Photograph by the author.)

USS *Rhode Island* (SSBN 740) arrives at the navy pier in Newport for a commissioning ceremony in July 1994. (U.S. Navy photograph by G.A. Saad.)

"Welcome to the Fleet . . . and to Rhode Island." The USS *Rhode Island* was commissioned in ceremonies on July 9, 1994, in Newport, Rhode Island. The submarine is shown during the commissioning event, with the Newport Bridge in the background. (U.S. Navy photograph by R.E. LaChance.)

Following commissioning at Newport, the nation's newest Trident Submarine, the USS *Rhode Island*, is on its way in Narragansett Bay to Long Island Sound and the open sea. (U.S. Navy photograph by G.A. Saad.)

USS *Rhode Island* philatelic cover. For the commissioning of the USS *Rhode Island* at Newport, an official envelope was prepared, bearing the ship's crest or logo in official colors. Shown here (in black and white) is a franked envelope with the special Commissioning Station imprint and postmark from Newport Post Office's Middletown Branch. (Author's collection.)

Historic Coasters Harbor Island. Looking south from the Naval War College across Dewey Field, one can see that the "O" Club—Commissioned Officers Club, Open (or COMO)—sits at the edge of the Naval Education and Training Center marina where sailing ships of the navy's training fleet once docked. Just beyond the Newport Bridge is the Newport Doubletree Hotel on Goat Island (in the background on the right), where in 1869 the navy first took up residence in Newport with the world's first experimental naval research facility. The navy has long since departed the site, and Goat Island is now linked by an automobile and pedestrian causeway to downtown Newport. (Photograph by the author.)

The flagpole in front of the Naval War College Museum (the building originally occupied by the Naval War College when it was founded in 1884). From this view, the present naval hospital complex can be seen across the marina. (Photograph by the author.)

Acknowledgments

Many of the views in this book were selected from original U.S. Navy photographs in the holdings of Newport navy commands. Some are from other navy sources, including the U.S. Navy Historical Center; the U.S. Naval Academy; the *Newport Navalog*, a nongovernment weekly published for the navy community; and the *NUSCOPE*, which was issued biweekly by the Naval Underwater Systems Center Public Affairs Office from 1970–1992.

The largest number of images come from the Naval War College Archives and Naval War College Museum in Newport, and are credited in the caption lines, as are other navy releases where photographers are cited. All released photographs from Newport commands, the U.S. Navy Historical Center, the U.S. Naval Academy, or other navy source were copied or scanned for use at no cost to the government.

Newport harbor scenes in chapter one appeared in W.A. Greene's *The Providence Plantations for Two Hundred and Fifty Years* (1886). The Naval Torpedo Station commanders' plaques mentioned in chapter one were photographed from a display at the Naval Undersea Warfare Center Division Newport. Credit for images in chapter two, except where otherwise noted, goes to Richard V. Simpson of the Bristol Art Exchange, who shared photographs and postcards from his collection, including those from his book-in-preparation, *The Torpedo Boats of Bristol, Rhode Island*. Naval Underwater Systems Center scenes in chapter six are U.S. Navy photographs from released selections compiled for the history of the center, *Meeting the Submarine Challenge*. Photographs by the author and by Darcy Associates, Ltd. are copyrighted.

It is a pleasure to acknowledge the cooperation of those who helped with archival material and loaned photographs for copying. Especially appreciated is the assistance of Evelyn Cherpak (archivist, Naval War College) and Director Anthony Nicolosi and Ruth Kiker of the Naval War College Museum. The U.S. Naval Academy Museum and Archives staff in Annapolis were helpful in locating photographs of the Civil War period when the academy moved to Newport. Similarly, Martha Mitchell of the John D. Rockefeller Library at Brown University went to considerable effort to research and copy items on Rhode Island's early naval patriots. For various courtesies and assistance with dates, the identification of ships and events, and advice on captions, thanks go to Jeffrey Owens, Gary Steigerwald, Gabriel Saad, Sandra Marceau, and James Mellin.